Copyright @ 2021 by John R. Brown and Brian J. Wright
ISBN: 978-1-5271-0701-4
Published by Christian Focus Publications Ltd
Geanies House, Fearn, Tain, Ross-shire IV20 1TW www.christianfocus.com

This edition published in 2021.
Cover illustration and internal illustrations by Lisa Flanagan
Cover and internal design by Lisa Flanagan
Printed and bound in Turkey

All rights reserved. No part of this publication may be reproduced, stored in a retrieval system, or transmitted, in any form, by any means, electronic, mechanical, photocopying, recording or otherwise without the prior permission of the publisher or a licence permitting restricted copying. In the U.K. such licences are issued by the Copyright Licensing Agency, 4 Battlebridge Lane, London, SE1 2HX. www.cla.co.uk

Obadiah & the Edomites

John Brown
Brian Wright

CF4·K

His name means "the Lord's servant." He was **a prophet**, someone chosen by God to deliver **God's messages** to **God's people.**

One day God showed Obadiah how he was going to punish Israel's neighbors, **the Edomites.** The Edomites had been mean to God's people, Israel, for a **very long time.**

It all started with twin brothers named **Jacob** and **Esau**.

Esau was born first, which meant he would get more of the family's property. But when he grew up, he sold his bigger share to his younger brother, Jacob, for a bowl of **red stew**. This foolish trade earned him the nickname "Edom," which means **"Red,"** which is why his family were called the **Edomites**.

Jacob's family was called **Israel**, which was the new name God gave Jacob. The Edomites and Israelites lived next to each other, and **they fought** a lot!

The Israelites served **the one true God**, but the Edomites created their own gods. The Edomites refused to be nice to the Israelites, which made God very angry. He does not like it when people mistreat his children.

But the Edomites didn't care, for they lived in a rock fortress high in the mountains called **Petra**, **"the Rock"**! They boasted, "No one can get us way up here!"

They were wrong, though, for their pride deceived them.

So God warned them,

"Even if you lived **as high as eagles** fly,
as high as stars in the sky,
even from way up there
I will bring you **crashing down!**"

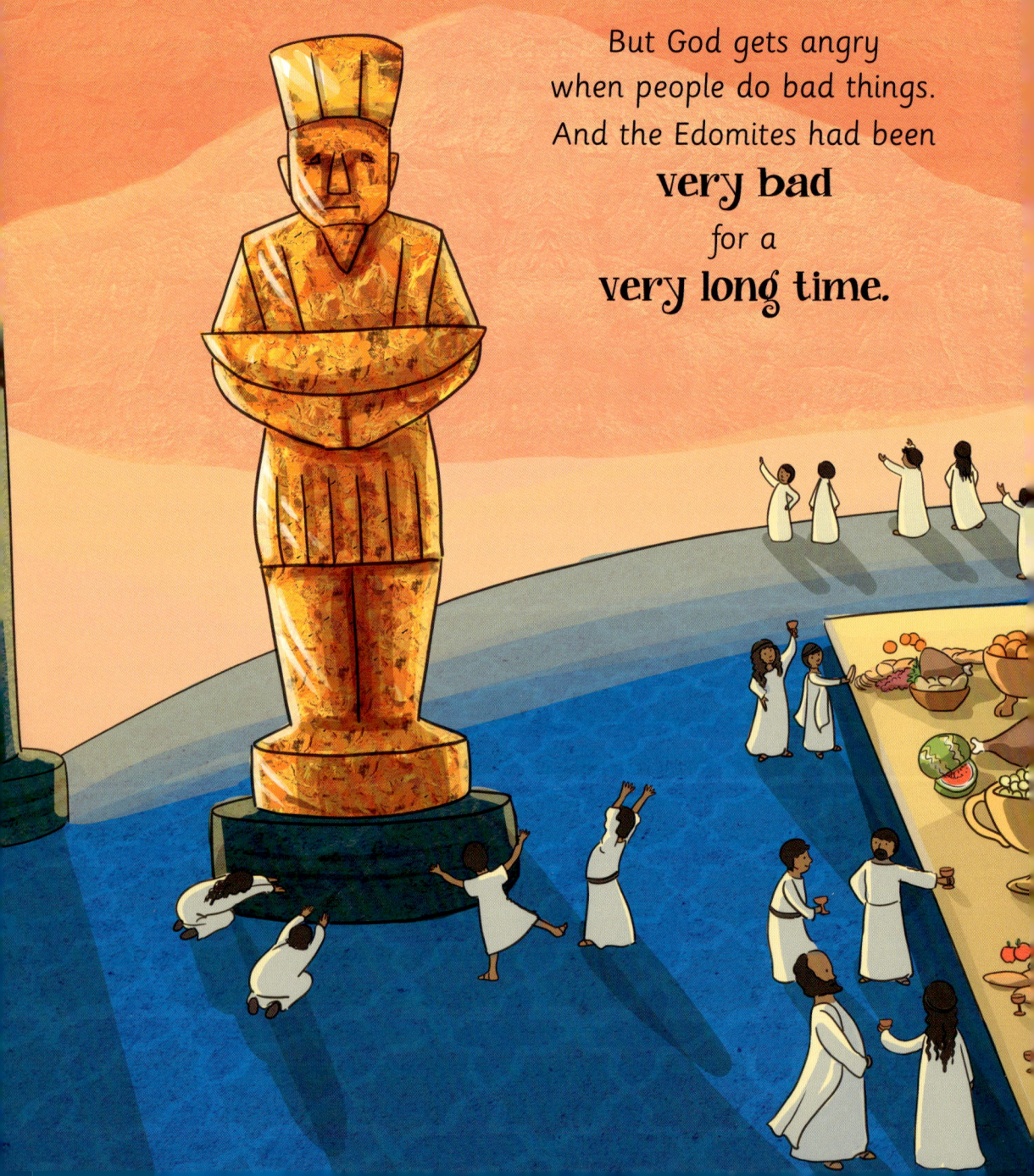

God had blessed the Edomites with a place to live, food to eat, and many good things to enjoy. But they weren't grateful. Instead **they rejected God** and mistreated his people.

But God gets angry when people do bad things. And the Edomites had been **very bad** for a **very long time.**

One time some mean people from Babylon (the same people who put Daniel's three friends in the fiery furnace) came to Israel and started **hurting God's people** and **stealing from God's temple.**

Did the Edomites come to help their relatives, the Israelites?

No! In fact, they laughed and made fun of them!

God wasn't laughing, though, and he told the Edomites to stop.
But did they listen to God? **No!**
They kept on laughing and teasing. Then it got worse.

The Edomites started stealing from Israel! "Stop stealing!" God told the Edomites through Obadiah.

But did they listen to God? **No!**

They kept on stealing. Then it got even worse.

The Edomites started hurting the Israelites! The Edomites took God's children and gave them to mean people. "Stop hurting my children!" God told the Edomites through Obadiah.

But did they listen to God? **No!**

They kept on hurting his children.

Can you believe all the bad things the Edomites did?

First, **they refused** to protect their relatives the Israelites.

Then **they laughed** at them.

Then **they stole** from them.

Then **they hurt** them and **took them away** from their home!

Can you imagine how angry they made God? **Israel** had also made God angry, for they were disobeying him as well. Therefore God's message to the Edomites was a warning to **the Israelites** too.

Obadiah warned that the Edomites' **pride** would be their **downfall,** for God doesn't like it when we think we're better than we are—especially when this leads us to **ignore** or **disobey** God!

So to **humble them,** God said he would take away everyone they trusted in instead of him.

Their friends would betray them.

Their teachers would be destroyed.

Their soldiers would be defeated.

The Edomites were in **BIG** trouble!

Then Obadiah shared some **good news** with Israel.

One day God will punish all the bad people and keep them from hurting anyone ever again.

At that time, God will bring all his children home to live together with him forever.

Best of all,
God himself will be King in that day!
King Jesus is coming to judge and to rule!
Everything will be perfect when King Jesus
rules God's people in **God's kingdom!**

Obadiah is the shortest book in the Old Testament, but it teaches some **great big lessons.**

Like the Edomites, **we're all proud** and need to humble ourselves before God.

Like the Edomites and Israelites, **we've all done bad things** that make God angry.

But if we ask God to forgive us
and trust in **his Son, King Jesus,** to be **our Savior,**
then we'll live with God forever someday.

Amen!

Christian Focus Publications publishes books for adults and children under its four main imprints: Christian Focus, CF4K, Mentor and Christian Heritage. Our books reflect our conviction that God's Word is reliable and Jesus is the way to know him, and live for ever with him.

Our children's publication list covers pre-school to early teens. We also publish personal and family devotional titles, biographies and inspirational stories that children will love.

From pre-school board books to teenage apologetics, we have it covered!

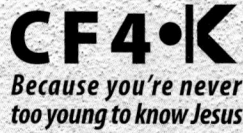

"Have you thought Obadiah was too hard for kids to understand? With clarity and biblical truth about Jesus in the Minor Prophets, Brian and John will convince you otherwise."
BARBARA REAOCH, former director of the Children's Division of Bible Study Fellowship International, and author of *A Better Than Anything Christmas* and *A Jesus Christmas*

"Too many people--kids and parents included—miss out on the rich truths of the Minor Prophets. I am happy to recommend Obadiah by Dr. Wright and Pastor Brown as a rich resource for families. This fresh look at an overlooked book will bless you and your children."
DIANNE JAGO, mother of three, founder of *Deeply Rooted Magazine*, and author of *A Holy Pursuit: How the Gospel Frees Us to Follow and Lay Down Our Dreams*

"In teaching our children, Christian parents and children's workers are always on the lookout for expressions of biblical truth that are clear, simple, and understandable. They do so with hopes and prayers that, in using these, our children will see more of the beauty of God and his word as they understand these better. What a joy and blessing to have now a resource that does just this with one of the parts of the Bible that may seem most distant for our children, but parts that, rightly understood, are tremendously relevant and life-impacting. Brian Wright and John Brown provide beautifully crafted and compelling renditions of the Minor Prophets in ways that we and our children can understand better the powerful message of these books of the Bible. They carefully uncover the ancient context of these messages while bringing them forward to our day, and in ways our children can understand. I have no doubt of the tremendous benefit these will prove to be for countless Christian parents and churches."
BRUCE A. WARE, Professor of Christian Theology, Southern Seminary, Louisville, Kentucky, and author of *Big Truths for Young Hearts*

"The entire Bible, even the section called the Minor Prophets, is relevant for God's people, including children. Kudos to the authors for making the Minor Prophets accessible to children through these illustrated, engaging summaries of each of the twelve books. After reading these summaries, children should come away knowing what each book is about, as well as the important principles God wants us to learn. I'm looking forward to reading this book to my grandsons in the days ahead."
ROBERT CHISHOLM, Chair and Senior Professor of Old Testament Studies, Dallas Theological Seminary, and author of *Interpreting the Minor Prophets* and *Handbook on the Prophets*